DEPARTMENT OF HEALTH AND SOCIAL SECURITY
DEVELOPMENT GROUP – SOCIAL WORK SERVICE

Records in Social Services Departments

"The personal social services are large-scale experiments in ways of helping those in need. It is both wasteful and irresponsible to set experiments in motion and omit to record and analyse what happens. It makes no sense in terms of administrative efficiency and, however little intended, it indicates a careless attitude towards human welfare."

Para 456, Seebohm Report 1968.

A Development Group Project Report

London: Her Majesty's Stationery Office

First published 1977

ISBN 0 11 320308 X

Contents

Editorial note

Acknowledgements to the social services departments who assisted in this project, to the DHSS Central Management Services Branch team who worked with the Development Group and to the Regional Social Work Service Officers are made in the main body of this report. Others who made valuable contributions were Social Work Service Officers at Headquarters, members of the Development Group, in particular Mrs Judy Downey who carried out the early project work and produced the first draft of the report, Miss Ruth Martin, a student with the Development Group, who followed up the issue of confidentiality, Mrs Lillien Davidson, formerly Principal Social Work Service Officer, London North Region, who revised the report prior to publication, and Miss Kahn, Chief Librarian DHSS for the production of the bibliography.

BARBARA KAHAN

Foreword

In times of severe economic stringency, it is more than ever essential that painful strategic choices should be based upon sound information about the need for and effectiveness of services. Current evidence suggests that many social services departments still do not have sufficient detailed and reliable data on which to base decisions about service priorities and changes of emphasis or expansion in one direction to compensate for reduction elswhere.

This lack of operational intelligence is partly due to an absence of adequate client records, and to the low degree of comparability of many of the records kept. For example, records maintained by one area of a large social services department may not readily be comparable with those in another because a different range of information is collected. Comparability between different social services departments is even less possible. Even nationally compiled statistics may be of doubtful authenticity if they are based upon differing interpretations of what is required.

The Social Work Service Development Group commenced this preliminary study of social services departments records towards the end of 1972. The report was not published when first prepared, partly because the Social Work Service had, by then, embarked upon a national Service Delivery Study which included examination of records and procedures in the selected areas. Then in 1974/5, the Social Work Service Residential Care study, complementary to the earlier exercise on Service Delivery, again included appraisal of records, this time relevant to clients in residential establishments.

All three projects, which span a period before and after local government reorganisation, nevertheless tell the same story of a continuing lack of basic data about clients to whom various services are offered and upon which judgements about policies and choices of service delivery can be made. The repetition of this evidence over a span of 4-5 years now prompts the issue of this Report and its recommendations. Although it describes work carried out mainly in 1973/4 its findings are still relevant, and based on what is believed to be a realistic appraisal of both evidence and possibilities. The recommendations are simple. Some may think them too simple; but experience suggests a search for elaborate perfection could prevent efforts to improve the current situation. Careful simplicity and an agreed basic minimum of recorded information may be better foundations from which to work in a period when staff and money are both in short supply.

The report draws attention to a chronic deficiency which can result in hit or miss decisions about social service provision to clients. If it were possible to implement its recommendations a contribution might be made not only to economy of effort, money and manpower, but most important of all, to clients who might receive better value from the resources currently available.

The Development Group was indebted to the social services departments who contributed material about records and those who were willing to be visited to discuss the problems at some length with members of the Group and colleagues from regional teams of Social Work Service. The continuing difficulties experienced in achieving adequate and suitable records as part of the essential tools to carry out social work and provide social services give evidence of the complexity of the problem.

The views expressed and the recommendations made in the report do not necessarily represent the policy of the Department of Health and Social Security or the local authorities and others who contributed.

Background to the project

1. In April 1972, the National Institute for Social Work convened a meeting to consider the desirability of setting up a national working party to help co-ordinate, study and make suggestions on local records and statistics in social services departments. Issues identified at the meeting were:

   a. the immediate need for standard and commonly agreed definitions for use in social services departments' records;
   b. the need for clearer information about cases at the local level;
   c. the need for improved recording of intake activities;
   d. the need to make social work plans, activities and results more explicit;
   e. the influence of both content and form of recording upon actual social work practice.

2. As a result, the meeting agreed that the Social Work Service Development Group of the Department of Health and Social Security should be asked as a matter of urgency to establish a working party on local records and statistics in social services departments, with local authority, central government, academic institutions and other interested groups represented upon it.

3. The implications of the original discussion would have been for a major project on records of all kinds in social service departments, but in the event it was considered desirable to commence with a more restricted brief i.e. a small project focussed on records needed at an initial stage and a second-stage document. The project was also asked to produce a possible check-list of the information required for such documents, which could be used by social services departments or voluntary organisations to initiate a case record for any type of case, together with a model document to illustrate one means of setting out the required information. As will be seen from the text of this report, even these aims needed modification in the light of the experience and information gathered as the project proceeded. The project work itself helped to indicate what proposals would be feasible at a time of developing complexity and variety of social services department structures and patterns of work.

4. Due to the large number and variety of voluntary organisations concerned with personal social services, it was decided with regret to

restrict investigation of current intake documentation and practice to a selection of local authority social services departments. These departments span the majority of situations of need and it was considered likely that if the outcome of the project was helpful to them it might also be helpful to voluntary organisations.

5. A large number of people contributed to the project in various ways. The Development Group gratefully acknowledges their help, particularly the members of the DHSS CPS4* team, who were asked to assist. This report owes much to their contribution.

Method of work

6. The project was planned in conjunction with the Regions and Headquarters of the Social Work Service and in consultation with other professional and administrative groups in DHSS. There was also continuous consultation with Directors and staffs at various levels in social services departments of differing size and geographical location. The National Institute for Social Work and the Brunel Institute of Organisation and Social Studies (Social Services Organisation Research Unit) gave valuable assistance.

7. At the outset the Development Group wrote to 35 Social Services Departments (listed in para 8) and requested samples of documents used during intake processes. These were chosen to give a geographical spread throughout the country, a balance between urban and rural areas and a selection of those social services departments which had undertaken work on records since 1971.

8. Social Services Departments asked to supply copies of intake documents (pre-1974 local government reorganisation):

1. Bradford
2. Cambridgeshire
3. Cheshire
4. Coventry
5. Devon
6. Hampshire
7. Hertfordshire
8. Kent
9. Lancashire
10. Leeds
11. Manchester
12. Newcastle
13. Norfolk
14. Oxfordshire
15. Portsmouth
16. Sheffield
17. Shropshire
18. Southampton

*Central Management Services Branch

8. *(Continued).*

19. Suffolk, East
20. Sussex, East
21. Sussex, West
22. Walsall
23. Worcestershire
24. West Riding
25. Bexley
26. Greenwich
27. Hammersmith
28. Harrow
29. Havering
30. Hillingdon
31. Kensington and Chelsea
32. Lewisham
33. Merton
34. Redbridge

9. Eleven local authorities were visited during the course of the project and correspondence and discussions took place with a wide range of social services staff.

10. Visits to local authority social services departments were planned and carried out with regional Social Work Service Officers wherever possible. Liaison was also established with DHSS Statistics and Research Branch 6*. A member of that branch accompanied the project team on three visits.

11. Documents received from 26 local authorities in response to the Development Group's request were analysed and the result used as a basis for discussion on visits to social services departments. During these visits in addition to "intake" documents, records relating to field work, residential day care, domiciliary services, liaison with services such as education and housing, and records needed for management, planning, financial and research purposes were discussed.

12. In addition, the Development Group had the advantage of access to material gathered by the Social Work Service in a national "Service Delivery Study". This study and some of the implications were written up by Miss Joan Cooper CB in the journal "Social Work Service" Issue No. 6 dated June 1975. An immense amount of material was collected in the Social Work Service regions regarding social services departments' records and this study has been freely drawn on in shaping the body of this report. Then, in 1974/5, Social Work Service undertook a "Residential Care Study". Aspects of this were written up in the journal "Social Work Service" No. 10 dated July 1976. That study emphasised and extended into the residential setting all the issues discussed in this project report.

*The Personal Social Services Statistics and Research Branch

13. Analysis of first 26 forms received from Social Services Departments: frequency with which items of information appeared on forms.

Client's name/surname	26
forenames	14
Name	25
Family name	8
Maiden name	1
Known as	1
Mr, Mrs, Miss	2
Sex – male or female	4
Sex	9
Address	26
Previous address	3
Usual address, if different	2
Address, if different	3
Telephone number	18
Date of birth/age	17
Place of birth	1
Origin, place of birth, year entered UK	2
Nationality, origin, year entered UK	3
Is client known/previous papers?	11
Referred by	26
Referred by address	8
Referred by telephone number	13
Relationship	2
How referred	14
Is client aware of referral?	8
Referral taken by	9
Presenting problem/request	12
Reason for referral	8
Marital status	10
Marital state	4
Married cohabiting dates	1

National insurance/other registration numbers	1
Legal solicitor/wills	1
Service in HM Forces	1
Occupation, school, training	7
Occupation, school	17
Working hours	1
Religion or creed	8
Religion	6
Baptised	1
Confirmed	1
Composition of household/family	25
Relationship to client	19
Next of kin name	6
Next of kin address	5
Next of kin telephone number	2
Next of kin relationship	1
Nearest relative	2
Putative father	1
Foster parents	1
Relatives non-household	2
Housing type	8
Housing tenant, owner occupied	5
Housing number of rooms	2
Housing landlord name	3
Housing landlord address	2
Housing notes	1
Living alone	1

13. *(Continued).*

GP	1
GP name	23
GP address	8
GP telephone number	11
GP notes	1
GP consulted	1
Disability/handicap	3
Health physical/mental handicaps	6
Hospital/homes admissions	2
Is handicap known to client?	1
Hospital consultant name	4
Hospital consultant address	2
Hospital consultant telephone number	1
Hospital visitor name	1
Hospital visitor telephone number	1
Hospital medical social worker name	1
Hospital medical telephone number	1
Hospital medical address	1
Finances	1
Finance income	5
Finance outgoings	4
Finance debts	2
Personal support available	1
Resources needed	1
Part III accommodation needed	1

Summary of problems	4
Brief outline of first contact	2
Diagnostic summary/assessment	5
Action taken/recommended	19
Objective/future plans	4
Services supplied by local authority	1
Services provided	3
Allocated to	14
Social work team	1
Senior social worker	2
Date of interview	1
Record of interview	1
Date	26
Time	7
Signature	12
Urgency of case	3
Other agencies	16
Other interested parties/individuals	3
Review date	2
Cross reference	1
Case record updated	1
Date case closed	2
Death	1
Number of copies/three	2
Number of copies/two	4
Number of copies not known	20

Definitions

14. The experience of the project showed little similarity between one local authority and another in the method by which information about clients was collected or processed and there was wide variation in the information required on forms currently in use. The argument that local needs were reflected in local documents was not substantiated by the evidence collected.

As no standardised terminology existed, it was not possible to make valid comparisons. Many of those who took their own definitions for granted were not aware of inherent contradictions or alternative

14. *(Continued).*
interpretations. Others had made choices between devising their own vocabulary, individually or in co-operation with other authorities, borrowing one already in use or awaiting the results of research either within their own department or elsewhere.

15. The term "referral" is an example of problems of definition. It is used to denote:

a. the first or initial contact or approach to a social services department;
b. the acceptance of this initial contact for further action;
c. a number of on-going activities involving the social services department (not necessarily the same as (b)).

16. There was also no generally accepted definition of the term "case" in the local authorities involved in the project; eg one local authority defined "case" as a situation in which "casework" was being carried out, and by implication assumed that someone receiving help under the Chronically Sick and Disabled Persons Act, 1970, was not a "case" in the same way as a parent or child or family being helped under the provisions of the Children and Young Persons Acts, 1963 and 1969.

17. Such interpretations can be an implicit way of rationing social workers' time and restricting demand from certain clients. Some clients classified as "cases" under children's legislation might benefit from material aid and domiciliary services while clients not classified as "cases" in this sense might benefit from "casework" as well as material aid.

18. A definition can also be used as a means of control as well as a means of rationing services. If a request for a home help or an aid or adaptation under the Chronically Sick and Disabled Persons Act, 1970 is accepted, for example, the implication may be that an available service eg home help, telephone etc terminates the case, despite the fact that this may be only part of the total need of the individual in question. Loneliness, poverty, eligibility for rate or rent rebate or free school meals for children may go undiagnosed and uninvestigated because of limited definitions.

19. The following examples from two local authorities further illustrate the problem: (our italics)

Example A

The following . . . . were not "regarded as *referrals* unless taken up as a *case* by the area:

a. police list of cautions;
b. housing rent arrears list;
c. notification of local authority children involved in offences in other police authorities;
d. notification of local authority children involved in offences in the local authority (normally where police are taking no action);
e. other similar lists;
f. information requests from other local authorities;
g. requests for lists of day minders, voluntary or private homes for the elderly, etc."

Example B

In analysing "referrals" (defined as "contacts with the social services department") under the heading "Summary of Action Taken" the following outcomes were possible:

"a. Visit made – becomes case –
b. Visit made – does not become case –
c. Visit made – does not become case – services not required
d. No visit made – does not become case – referral dealt with
e. No visit made – does not become case – referred to other agency (including other area teams)
f. No visit made – does not become case – services not available
g. No visit made – no decision on becoming case, awaiting social worker's visit."

(A note indicated that the last category should only be used in the exceptional circumstances of a delay of 10 weeks or more between referral and visit by social worker.)

Records in social services departments

20. Records in social services departments potentially perform many functions. At the simplest level they can provide an account of the agency's contact with a client – when it occurred, who the client was and what services he received. Their aim is to enable the social services department and all staff within it to render the best possible service without overlapping, loss of the client's identity or mutually time-wasting verbal repetition of data on each contact. However, there are also more sophisticated views of the value of records. For example, in a society which is both mobile and predominantly literate, records can help with problems of memory and identity. This is especially important for children spending part of their life in care, for those who have suffered severe mental or physical illnesses and for elderly whose memory can be assisted by recorded fact. On a different level, records can be analysed to demonstrate how and where public resources have been deployed, or to assist future planning.

21. Records are also needed to facilitate communication and procedures between the different activities of a social services department. There are many situations in which individuals may be dependent on the accuracy and reliability of records of facts, decisions, queries, concern and actions on their behalf. Clients often envisage different agencies as part of an overall communicating and interacting structure, not appreciating the intricate and complex procedures necessary to ensure communication and co-ordination between services.

22. Records can help to contribute to decisions about the allocation of resources. Without them, priorities have to be settled in the absence of knowledge on whether existing services meet existing demands, or what additional or different services are required. If, as a result, some decisions seem remote and insensitive, it may be because information on which to base "better" judgements is not available.

23. Since 1970 many research and intelligence posts have been created in social services departments, and there has been greater interest and involvement in the collection and utilisation of information, particularly in relation to attempts to base planning on factual

23. *(Continued).*
material. This has been encouraged by new forms of management in local government. The development of corporate planning, for example, implies that each chief officer needs accurate and up-to-date information about the work and resources of his department, and some social services departments have already felt they suffered by comparison with other parts of their authority through a lack of "hard" information about clients, costs, alternative ways of providing services and the impact they make on demand, and the extent of "unmet need".

24. Central government, too, has emphasised the importance of well informed planning techniques both in the short and the long-term, for capital programme, manpower and service planning and expects local authorities and other services to co-operate. Cuts in public expenditure increase the pressures for accurate and comparable information on workloads, demand, services provided, and ratios of staff to cases and population in order to justify the allocation of resources. A realistic and appropriate distribution of limited resources will depend on adequate information. The development of computer technology has reinforced these trends.

25. It must, however, be plainly stated that there is a good deal of ambivalence and some confusion in relation to records. Some senior professionals both in central and local government, and others who are not carrying out direct social work functions, make certain assumptions concerning the records kept by social services departments and their uses; different assumptions may be made by social services management personnel, research workers and other local authority departments. The administrative structure of a social services department may reinforce existing assumptions or ignore them in different ways.

26. Social workers are also often unsure about the purpose and appropriate form of records and their own involvement in the recording process. At one extreme, records may be regarded as a privately kept personal note of a continuing relationship; sometimes they are tolerated as an administrative incursion necessary "to keep the books straight". At the other extreme, they may be regarded as unnecessary interference with the task of the social worker, and serving "irrelevant" purposes, such as statistics, research or planning.

27. In several of the local authorities visited, a degree of priority had been given to work on records but often pressure for change had come from a point too low down in the power structure (eg the systems analyst or the research officer) for it to be enforceable or to carry the necessary weight. In the process of decentralisation and devolution of responsibility to area teams, some social services departments had not emphasised that methods of recording should not be part of this process and a number of area teams appeared to feel that it was part of their role to design records and forms and be free to deviate from those which were centrally designed.

28. Some social services departments had invested considerable expenditure on personnel and equipment in developing new or improving existing systems. Working parties involving social workers at all levels had been set up and their suggestions and amending proposals had been incorporated. This kind of joint activity had often led to the positive involvement of all concerned.

29. Many with experience of deciding what records are necessary, considered that the general policy of a social services department, whatever it happened to be, and the type of service the department intended to offer, needed to be widely known within the departmental structure. This was considered important, partly on grounds of efficiency and good communications and partly for reasons of equity in the treatment of requests for help or information.

Need for comparable information

30. This project proceeds on the assumption that there is value for the client, the agency and society in general if social services departments record a minimum amount of comparable basic information concerning clients and services. This is not the same thing as prescribing universal methods of recording information and it is important to make this distinction at the outset. Social services departments are each differently managed, serviced and staffed and it is not practicable to assume that a common records system is likely to be adopted. On the other hand, collection of comparable information might have many benefits for individual departments and for personal social services as a whole.

31. At present, on all the evidence available, it would be difficult for many directors of social services to state how many people in a year have asked their departments for help, who referred them, why they came, and whether or not they were known to other agencies who might have relevant information about them. Even where such information is collected, reliable and up-to-date, a director cannot compare his situation with other local authorities, since information other than national statistics is not generally assembled in comparable form either between local authorities or even, sometimes, within parts of the same local authority.

32. The reasons for advocating the collection of standard (and therefore comparable) information are as follows:

a. clients might receive a better service;
b. equitable treatment of clients might be assisted;
c. continuity of treatment might be more effectively organised;
d. there might be less waste of time in scanning casefiles for a variety of purposes;
e. tasks of specialists, advisers and consultants might be facilitated;
f. transfer of information within, and where necessary between, local authorities might be easier;
g. there might be more effective organisation and control of workloads;
h. a valuable contribution might be made to management and training, because procedures and roles could be clarified;
i. extraction of data for statistical and research purposes might be more reliable.

33. In much of the literature on recording, the objective of providing a basis for comparability is rarely mentioned. There are many subtle rationalisations for this. Someone commented in relation to a plea for a national standard system of case recording: "Heaven forbid! Each case and each caseworker is unique . . . . ."

M E Stockbridge* reacted to this:

> "Now if clients (and social workers) are wholly unique it is clear that not only standardisation but also generalisation is impossible and that we should therefore despair of ever developing any theory.

*"Social Case Recording", Case Conference, December 1968, Vol XV, No. 8.

33. *(Continued).*

In fact, while clients and social workers are individuals, they have a great deal in common: for example, they all have a date of birth, a significant proportion work, are married, have children, occupy houses; all are the product of a male and female parent and most can identify them; all have been children and so on.

If data can be ordered it can be compared and then the truly unique, or the exceptional circumstance, is much more likely to be discernible. As to fearing that the setting of a standard will result in lack of motivation to surpass the minimal acceptable level, I see no reason to assume that social workers are any less motivated than, say surgeons, who continuously develop new techniques for "standard operations" but who are much more prepared to communicate their ideas for improvements to their colleagues. There is a danger that the uniqueness issue can become a defence against the acceptance of any professional discipline".

First contacts with the client

34. A detailed examination of the way in which social services departments receive their clients and allocate their services, from the first point of contact to the point at which a decision is made to provide a service or take some other action, was part of the process of the Service Delivery Study. A wide divergence of practice was revealed. To some extent this diversity sprang from the lack of agreed definitions of the various steps of the process (see paras 14-19). To some extent it was the result of sheer expediency or pressures of the moment (eg when no record was kept). This lack of records cannot be dismissed as mere aberration, since it springs from the realities of staff shortages, heavy workloads, insufficient training etc. Yet again, there were sometimes tacit assumptions that each worker made decisions ad hoc as to the nature and extent of recording. What became clear when all the material from the Study was compared with the detailed analysis of 26 documents collected by the Development Group from social services departments was that the terms "first stage" and "second stage" in the terms of reference of the Records Project introduced ambiguity and endless fuel for argument. When is a "first stage" ended? What does a "second stage" imply?

35. As a result of the different systems and techniques, initial contact with and reception of a client are often not readily distinguishable from the next stage and in some situations and local authorities, they form part of the same activity. In others, they are separate systems and involve the client being seen by a receptionist who may record some identifying information. Further investigation is then carried out by a social worker to decide whether the case is appropriate to the social services department. Some systems involve an "intake team", ie a group of social workers who attend to all new clients and work with them for the first few weeks or longer, if it appears that need can be met without long-term commitment of social work time. If the necessity for long-term commitment is established, the case is passed to other social workers for further action.

36. The amount of information recorded in the early stages may be determined by a number of factors:

a. the procedure adopted by the social services department eg "duty officer", "receptionist", "intake team" or none;
b. the type of form used;
c. the method of initial contact;
d. the condition and personality of the client or caller;
e. the client's point of entry and/or the reception area; eg the barriers to be overcome before reaching it; its characteristics in terms of physical condition, personnel, and degree of privacy;
f. the assessment at the first contact point of the appropriateness of the approach and whether this is recorded;
g. the assessment of the first interview of the amount of information necessary to decide the next or future action;
h. the amount of time the member of staff can expend in preparing a record.

37. At present, practice in intake procedures and decisions based on them varies widely both within and between local authorities. An interviewing officer (whether social worker, receptionist or clerk) may decide that the social services department cannot respond in a particular case and that another department of central or local government, or a voluntary agency, is more appropriate. Alternatively the client may decide not to take the matter further.

38. Whatever system is adopted, the referral of a client to a social services department starts a process of events which leads to a decision about the need for action at once or at some time in the future. In any event reception or intake information is likely to affect all future outcome.

39. Because of the different interpretations given to terms such as "referral" "intake", "reception" "first stage", "second stage" etc., these terms are not used in this report. Instead the term "The Client Personal Record" is used. This is intended to distinguish any document carrying personal details from a numerical count of clients or actions, which may be prescribed by management as an alternative or addition to the personal record. (See paras 53 and 54 regarding the question of inclusion or exclusion of contracts from the Client Personal Record system.)

The purposes of the client personal record

40. Information included in the Client Personal Record can serve the following purposes;

a. establish the client's eligibility for service;
b. help preserve his sense of identity and demonstrate that the social services department values his individuality even though he may have to relate to different workers and different branches of the department's work;
c. save time for client and worker by avoiding wasteful verbal repetition of data and history;
d. identify resources needed to provide services to clients;
e. provide a record of service rendered;
f. assess the extent to which needs have been met or not met;
g. evaluate the effectiveness of service given;
h. record information of value to the client either immediately or in the future;
i. provide a record of demands made on the social services department;
j. assist in staff supervision and training;
k. assist management and accountability processes;
l. inform planning processes;
m. serve as a base for statistics and research.

Factors which help determine content of record

41. In deciding the content of a record or records designed to meet the above objectives, it is necessary to consider:

a. the purposes for which the document will be used;
b. the degree of comprehensiveness which is practicable;
c. the procedures to be employed to ensure its appropriate use;
d. the contents necessary to achieve the purpose(s);
e. the people who will have access to it and its contents;
f. the client's participation in or knowledge of:
   i. What information is collected?
   ii. The uses to which it is put;
g. the stages of the recording process at which it will be relevant;
h. the parts of the social services organisation in which it will be used;
i. the other parts of the local authority organisation which will have access to it or its contents;
j. the other agencies or persons who will have access to it or its contents;
k. the ease of retrieval while in current use;
l. the method of updating;
m. the process of storage and retrieval when no longer in current use or after closure;
n. the stage at which the document is destroyed.

42. Such considerations also help to clarify the purposes of the document and the administrative procedures and organisational structure it is to serve.

43. At present many forms (some of which duplicate or overlap each other) are in use. In fact, the sheer volume of documents in social services departments presents an enormous organisational problem. Some departments have several hundred different forms in use. Social work and distribution of social services inevitably involve considerable documentation. This is implicit in the wide range of clients, services and establishments, in professional methods, and in the accountability and bureaucratic systems which these and the expenditure of public resources necessarily involve. But the forms have often been produced piecemeal to meet the needs of different

43. *(Continued).*
parts of professional and administrative structures, without incorporating their separate objectives into a coherent whole. For example, admission to residential care may involve several departments or sectors of a local authority, each of which requires a record of the admission for different purposes. To meet these requirements some departments have developed separate forms for financial, administrative and social work purposes. Unhappily the weight of documentation often serves only to deter the worker who is expected to complete the forms.

44. In the course of the project, it was noted that some local authorities which were re-designing their documents (including those relating to first contacts of clients with the department) were repeating questions which had appeared on previous forms from different settings without the reasons for doing so being clear. In many cases there were uncertainties about the uses which would be made of answers to questions, either by the social services department or other parts of the local authority.

45. Perhaps it is useful to pause and note that not all people who approach a social services department are asking for a service. A significant number are offering help. The method of dealing with these offers varies both between social services departments and within them, but none of those visited appeared to use purpose-designed forms. Some used, as far as possible, the same forms as those for clients seeking help, whilst others relied on a scrap pad or their memory to set procedures in motion.

46. Turning back to the main problems of identifying essential basic data, procedures varied a great deal in the local authorities involved in the project, in relation to the extent of recording, the form of recording or whether any record at all was made when a client first came to the notice of a social services department. Documents could include:

a. a "referral" form;
b. an "initial contact" form;
c. an "initial investigation report";
d. a "case record front sheet";
e. an "action document";

46. *(Continued).*

f. a financial assessment form;
g. assessment and diagnosis reports;
h. medical information;
i. social background information;
j. specialist information;
k. correspondence related to "referral"/"intake" and suggestions concerning necessary treatment or resources.

47. Documents received from local authorities clearly illustrated the great variety of approaches which existed under a general "intake" heading. Analysis* of 26 of these intake forms exemplified the type of information currently being recorded. They had only 4 items in common: the client's surname, address, source of referral and the date, but altogether there were 110 differently identified items of information and a wide range of names given to the forms themselves. These titles add some weight to the view that the heading of the form itself determines the content in the light of the worker's interpretation of it.

48. To illustrate this point the names of the 26 forms analysed are listed below:

Referral
Case referral
Referral form (2)
Case referral form (2)
Initial referral form
Initial referral
New referrals
Referral sheet and case front
Referral/record form
Enquiry form
Initial enquiry
Initial enquiry form (2)
Intake form
Case record
Request for assistance or advice
Case file front cover
Top sheet
Adult – (Case sheet 2)
Particulars of family
Key
No title or heading (3)

49. As already noted in earlier sections of this report, it is seldom possible to record all relevant facts at an early stage in a social services department's relationship with a client. Nor are there very many cases where either facts or problems remain constant. But it seems essential that a basic core of data should be collected as soon as practicable. Attention has therefore been given first to a checklist

*See para 13 page 4

49. *(Continued).*
of information to be quickly collected on all clients. The attempt to formulate "first stage" and "second stage" documents was abandoned. Commentaries received on drafts of these demonstrated all too plainly the ambiguities and misunderstandings this terminology created.

50. The original remit to the Development Group included a request to provide a checklist of information applicable to any type of case and to design a model form. As the project proceeded it became apparent that no single list or form could include all the information necessary for all types of case. Some clients and groups of clients require very detailed information on their social and family circumstances, their physical or mental capacities and special needs. Early efforts to draft a "universal" checklist embodied in a model form were rightly criticised on the grounds of being unwieldy, difficult to use, difficult to adapt to individual management systems and wasteful. Efforts to produce a model form for universal application were therefore also abandoned.

51. This did not, however, lead to the conclusion that the project was fruitless. Indeed, the reverse appeared true, in that it became more important to winnow out a basic core of data – a minimum, which all might agree to be necessary as a step towards standard (and therefore comparable) information.

Proposed minimum common basic data

52. The first proposal of this report is that a checklist should be agreed of common basic data to be collected for clients as an important step towards comparability within each social services department and eventually between all social services departments. Upon this minimum other information relevant to each case and management system could then be built.

53. To do this managements will have to decide *when* the Client Personal Record, containing this basic minimum, should be set up. Staff need to know, and to have guidelines in writing concerning which categories of client contact will qualify for inclusion and what criteria are to be applied. For example, callers wrongly directed to

53. *(Continued).*

the social services department might be excluded from the Personal Record system and dealt with instead by a numerical count; lists received from other agencies may not be included en bloc; people given brief information at the counter may not be included. Considerations of practicability and purposes served, plus a sound analysis of what happens at present will help to establish criteria. Of course, if it were possible for all social services departments to agree the criteria for inclusion and exclusion so much the better. But adoption of a basic minimum checklist for identified categories need not await the outcome of such refined debate on a national scale. Current practice during the course of the project and the Social Work Service national studies demonstrated that at present all contacts are not recorded, whether deliberately or by default. It is suggested that a record of some sort needs to be kept for *all* contacts, if only to illuminate the use of staff time, but these specific recommendations relate to the creation of a Client Personal Record on the basis of agreed criteria and incorporating an AGREED MINIMUM CORE OF BASIC DATA.

54. These points need to be stressed since otherwise it might wrongly be assumed that by advocating exclusion of certain groups from the Client Personal Record, this report was advocating no record at all for them. If no record is kept, management loses important information and in fact a form of "service rationing" may take place. How far such techniques of exclusion are explicit is not clear, but they can have an important effect on practice, attitudes and resource allocation. For example, several social services departments claimed to have very large numbers of "short term" cases. One stated that 30,000 out of 40,000 cases were "short term" and needed no further involvement. There was insufficient information to prove or disprove this argument.

Checklist of data to be recorded for all clients included in the client personal record system (CPR system)

55. Given that management has set out the criteria and arranged to monitor in some other way clients not included in the CPR system, the following checklist of minimum basic information is proposed.

1.	Date:	Day, month, year
2.	Name:	Surname, forename(s)
3.	Address and telephone number (or call box number, if possible)	Directions to get there if relevant, recent previous address(es)
4	Date of birth:	Day, month, year (not age)
5.	Sex:	Male/female
6.	Marital status:	Married/single/widowed/ divorced/separated/cohabiting
7.	Referred by:	Self/relative/friend/neighbour/ other person/agency; name(s), address(es), phone number(s)
8.	Method of referral:	Letter or other written communication/court/telephone call/visit/verbal communication other than telephone call
9.	Nature of request/ information given:	
10.	Whether client already known to Social Services Department	Yes/no/not known

Suggestions for additional information to be obtained when relevant

56. Information additional to the basic minimum will then depend upon individual circumstances and case development. However, there is a range which may be described as "case management information" which will almost certainly be desirable however brief or prolonged the contact, eg:

Case Management Information
- to whom client allocated;
- action taken, with dates;
- communications received and made, with dates;
- services/resources required;
- indications of degree of urgency;
- by whom, where and when services/resources provided;
- checks confirming satisfactory service provision;
- failure to provide service, with reasons;
- to which other agencies/persons case referred, with dates;
- review dates (statutory or otherwise);
- discussions with senior/supervisory staff (dates and content);
- summary and review of case (periodic/final).

This list might well become part of the agreed basic minimum.

57. Depending on clients' needs and problems, a range of additional personal material may need recording, when relevant – eg:

Additional Relevant Client Information
- other members of household;
- next of kin, relatives, friends;
- ethnic origin; language preferred;
- other interested agencies;
- housing;
- health information (including handicaps);
- financial information (including state benefits);
- education;
- employment;
- periods in social services department/voluntary/private residential establishments;
- periods in care (children and young persons).

57. *(Continued).*

– court appearances (dates);
– court orders (dates and content);
– nature of intermediate treatment and dates;
– special communication problems (eg speech, hearing);
– mobility problems.

These broad headings would need to be broken down into detail for specific purposes.

Some problems of recording

58. Despite the stated aims and objectives of many social services departments, records were not being used to facilitate communication and procedures between field and residential workers. The gap currently existing between them is still very great. It may exist even where local authorities are sensitive to and aware of problems in communication between field and residential staff. Yet they appear to have been unable to overcome them and often do not seem to attach much importance to records in residential work. This practical lack of interest in recording in relation to residential work is also apparent in the literature on social work recording.*

59. In the social services departments visited in the project, new recording systems had often been designed and introduced without any consultation with residential staff. It appeared that this was a continuation of previous practice before 1970 relating to the respective roles of residential and field social workers, which seldom allowed for communication between the two to be part of the normal procedural channels for which new documentation was intended.

60. In some local authorities it was explained that the difference in status between residential and field work staff precluded the sharing of information. Field workers it was often said regarded clients in residential care as still 'their' cases and consequently the information concerning them was theirs too. This was said despite the fact that there may have been little evidence of continuing relationships between field social workers and clients in a residential setting.

*e.g. Professor Noel Timms at no point refers to the needs of residential social work in "Recording in Social Work", 1972.

Records of clients in residential care

61. The Social Work Service Residential Care Study found the position on records remarkably uniform. Good administrative records were kept but poor records on personal histories and reviews. There were exceptions where standards were higher but the general picture was one of straightforward records relating only to matters such as admission, discharge, drugs, fire drills, medication, diets or punishment, according to the client group. In children's homes the Community Homes Regulations applied but these were not always complied with fully.

62. There was very little in the way of personal records relating to the elderly or the mentally handicapped, although records for the mentally ill contained rather more detail. Within the children's homes there was considerable variation between homes in different authorities but some kind of continuing record of each child was kept, and in most cases there were at least six monthly review records, although of varying quality.

63. Almost without exception there were complaints in homes for the elderly about the inadequacy of the records at the time of admission and in many cases these appeared to be justified. In some cases information accompanying a new resident was minimal. Records in area offices often appeared to be much more adequate than those in residential homes. This is a matter which requires examination by authorities, for apart from hindering the task, the result was a feeling on the part of heads of homes of being treated as second class citizens who were not entitled to information about people with whom they lived and for whom they had to care.

Storage and confidentiality of records

64. Many local authorities are concerned about the safety of personal information when it is stored in a digital format, processed by computer and handled by staff other than those in social services departments. Some local authorities try to overcome this problem by elaborate systems of coding or by using computers only for aggregated information. It is important to note, however, that similar concern is not always shown for the storage of information by manual systems where documents may be visible to the public or easily accessible to them. [A separate note on confidentiality is included in this Report (Appendix A).]

Systems of recording

65. A great deal of attention has been devoted to the development of new systems in recent years. Many local authorities and social services departments have planned or implemented new methods for the collection, storage and retrieval of information and documentation. Some of these have involved working groups of management, social workers and research staff. The methods include:

a. Manual processes; some local authorities have discarded previous manual systems, rejected computerisation as unsuitable and developed manual systems using edge punched cards, feature cards and other systems of this type.
b. Semi-automatic systems; these involve the use of 80 column punched cards which require a punch, a sorter and a tabulator.
c. Automatic data processing (ADP); this can involve the storage of client data in a central computer, which produces the required information about clients and workloads at frequent intervals in a printed format.

66. Some local authorities have planned visual display terminals and "interrogating keyboards" at area offices so that information on clients can be received immediately from the central computer. The information in the central computer can thus be updated directly from the area office or separately. In other cases, the computer does not supply any individual data, its main purpose being to produce statistics and management information.

67. There have inevitably been problems in the introduction of computer systems. The costs involved in terms of manpower and the need for accurate basic information have not always been appreciated throughout organisations. Computers depend as much on collection of relevant data as manual and semi-automatic systems. Nevertheless the trend seems to be towards increasing use of computers, and it is therefore desirable that individual local authorities should have a basis for comparability which is applicable to both manual and automatic systems.

The status of recording

68. In order to ensure adequate recording systems organisations have to make an explicit commitment to the value of this use of manpower and resources. This can be demonstrated in a number of ways, including the priority given to the activity and the attitude of management to its importance. If recording is not made a clear priority throughout an organisation, groups of staff may continue to produce their own variations on the system without realising the implications of their unilateral activities. In a working situation of pressure and complexity, it is inevitable that resistance to standardised recording will develop unless managers and social workers are supported in emphasising record-keeping as a vital part of the process.

General conclusions and recommendations

69. Record keeping is an essential element of the work of social services departments for reasons which include obligations to clients and the need of management for data upon which sound decisions can be based.

70. Evidence available not only from the work of this Records Project (1972/3) but also from the Social Work Service studies on Service Delivery (1973/4) and Residential Care (1974/5) suggests there is, in general, a lack of adequate and comparable client records. This deprives management of indispensable tools for use in planning, line management, staff supervision, development and training. It militates against sensitive client service and can erode the client's sense of identity and self-worth. It can lead to misdirection of scarce resources.

71. To some extent this situation is due to the specialised terminology in use in the social services world and the varying interpretations given to words like "referral", "case", "intake" and so on. This leads to lack of comparability of information collected, and contributes to workers' scepticism about the value of spending time keeping records.

72. A record should be kept for all types of client contact whether personal, written or verbal. In some instances this may be a numerical count; in others (to be determined by management) a Client Personal Record should be set up (paras 39 and 40).

73. Whatever system is decided upon, it should be uniform throughout the social services department, supported by top management policy and promulgated by written guidance readily available to all grades of staff.

74. Considerations of usefulness and comparability should determine the content of the Client Personal Record. The report suggests a checklist of data to be recorded for all clients included in this system (para 53).

75. It also suggests a checklist of case management information (para 56) and a range of additional relevant client information (para 57) to be collected according to needs and problems.

76. All client personal records, whether or not destined for computer systems, should be treated as confidential. Storage of all personal records should be secure from those who have no right to see them. The material collected should, in any event, be the minimum consistent with meeting specified objectives.

77. The complexities of social services terminology often bedevil efforts to achieve comparability. Too many and too elaborate forms deter workers from completing them, especially if the interpretation of terms used is unclear.

78. A separate issue is that of facilitating exchange of information between different staff groups (especially field and residential social workers) with the aim of rendering better services to clients without breaching the basic tenets of confidentiality.

79. All these issues could well benefit from discussion in a nationally convened forum, whose membership would command the respect of the various groups composing social services departments. Early recommendations on the adoption of a Client Personal Record containing simple, comparable information could be the first goal of such a forum. A dictionary or glossary of social services terminology would also be a useful outcome. Guidelines on the exchange of information between staff groups could assist in clarifying roles and perhaps contribute to more productive professional co-operation.

Finally, a measure of national agreement as to the purpose, nature and value of records might help staff overcome the natural antipathy felt by most people when asked to complete yet another form. To the extent that the present multiplicity of different record forms, the varying interpretation of terms and lack of comparability represents much wasted effort, it appears that any time spent in simplification and rationalisation would be an economy.

APPENDIX A

Note on confidentiality

During work on the Records Project, the question of confidentiality of social service client records was raised in various ways. Fears were expressed that, by working towards the greater degree of comparability advocated in the report, departments might be opening the door to misuse of the information collected. These anxieties seemed most acute when computers were in use, or proposed, for local authority data processing. It was pointed out to the project team that access to computerised material is quite legitimate for many people unconnected with social work–eg research staff, finance officers, training personnel. If personal material remains identifiably linked with the client, it is possible for it to be used without his knowledge or consent for purposes outside his original intention and even to his detriment.

It seemed right to give special consideration to these anxieties. Various references throughout the text of this report emphasise the importance of observing the basic tenets of confidentiality, whatever may be the chosen method of keeping and storing records or their level of comparability.

Two fairly recent publications examine these issues extensively, dealing with different but overlapping aspects of them. These are:

a. *Confidentiality in Social Work* revised edition 1976–published by the British Association of Social Workers.

b. *Computers and Privacy* White Paper Cmd 6353–published by HMSO. Presented to Parliament Dec 1975.

Of the considerable literature on this subject, the Seebohm Report (Report of the Committee on Local Authority and Allied Personal Social Services HMSO Cmd 3703 1968) had much to say which is still relevant to developments since its recommendations were put into effect by the Local Authority Social Services Act 1970.

Besides these three references, the short selection which follows and which represents different viewpoints on confidentiality may be useful to those who wish to pursue further reading on the substance of the Records Project report.

1. *Report of the Committee on Privacy* (Chairman: K. Younger). HMSO Cmnd. 5012 1972.

2. *Social Work Support for the Health Service.* Report of the Working Party (Chairman: G. J. Otton). HMSO 1974.

3. *Report of the Committee of Inquiry into the Care and Supervision provided in relation to Maria Colwell* (Chairman: T. G. Field-Fisher). HMSO 1974.

4. *Report of the Committee of Inquiry into the provision and co-ordination of services to the family of John George Auckland*. HMSO 1975.

5. Murch M. *Privacy – no concern of social work?* Social Work Today; Vol. 2 No. 5, 3 June 1971.

6. Smith, J. *The Auckland Case.* New Society; 27 November 1975.

7. Barter, J. *Putting it on the Record.* New Psychiatry; Vol. 2 No. 3, 30 January 1975.

8. Alexander, A. *How much should a Councillor know?* Community Care; 28 May 1975.

9. Tilley, G. *Confidentiality and records–a personal view.* The Community Home School Gazette; June 1975.

10. Mill, J. S. *On Liberty.* First published 1859.

11. Forder, A. *Social Casework and Administration.* Faber and Faber, 1968.

12. McDermott (Editor). *Self-determination in social work.* Routledge and Kegan Paul, 1970.

13. Mayer and Timms, *The Client Speaks.* Routledge and Kegan Paul, 1970.

Bibliography

Acheson, E. D., 1967 *Medical record Linkage.* London. Oxford University Press.

Acheson, E. D., editor, 1968. *Record Linkage in medicine; proceedings of the international symposium,* Oxford, July 1967. Edinburgh and London, Livingstone.

Advisory Council on Social Work, 1974. *Interim report of the Committee on Social Work Statistics.* Edinburgh, Advisory Council on Social Work, Committee on Social Work Statistics.

Alderson, M. R., 1973. *Health and Social Service Journal,* 83, 1524.

Ashley, J. S., 1972. *British Journal of Preventive and Social Medicine,* 26, 135.

Barter, J., 1975. *New Psychiatry,* 2, (3), 14.

Benjamin, B., 1973. *Journal of Social Policy*, 2, (1), 13.

Bristol, M. C., 1938. *Handbook of social case recording.* (Social Service Monographs No. 4) Chicago , University of Chicago Press.

British Association of Social Workers, 1972. *A code of ethics for social work.* (Discussion Paper No. 2) London. British Association of Social Workers.

British Association of Social Workers, 1976. *Confidentiality in social work.* Birmingham. British Association of Social Workers.

Carver, V. and Edwards, J. L., 1972. *Social workers and their workloads: report of an investigation into work time and work patterns of 572 social work personnel.* London. National Institute for Social Work Training.

Central Council for Education and Training in Social Work, 1973. *Training for residential work: discussion document. A new pattern suggested by the Working Party on Education for Residential Social Work. (Chairman D. M. Allen) with implications for training and education in the entire social services field.* London, Central Council for Education and Training in Social Work.

Central Health Services Council, 1965. *Report of the Sub-Committee of the Standing Medical Advisory Committee on the Standardisation of Hospital Medical Records.* (Chairman: R. E. Tunbridge) London, H.M.S.O.

Chea, M. W., 1972. *Social Casework,* **53**, 177.

Committee on Local Authority and Allied Personal Social Services. *(Seebohm Committee Report)* 1968. (Cmnd. 3703) London, H.M.S.O.

Davies, B., 1972. *Planning resources for personal social services:* the *James Seth Memorial Lecture 1971.* Edinburgh, University of Edinburgh, Department of Social Administration.

Davies, B., Barton, A. and McMillan, 1., 1972. *Variations in children's services among British urban authorities: a causal analysis.* (Occasional Paper on Social Administration No. 45) London. Bell.

Davies, B. P., et al., 1971. *Variations in services for the aged: a causal analysis.* (Occasional Paper on Social Administration No. 40) London, Bell.

Department of the Environment, 1974. *Local Government Act 1972: local authority records in England.* (Circular 17/74) London, Department of the Environment.

Department of Health and Social Security, 1972. *Local authority social services: 10 year development plans 1973-1983.* (Circular 35/72) London, D.H.S.S.

Department of Health and Social Security, 1977. *Forward Planning of Local Authority Social Services.* (LASSL (77)13) London, D.H.S.S.

Derbyshire, M. E., 1974. *A comparison of five computerised information systems in social services departments.* Preston, Lancashire County Social Services Department, Research Section.

Durrant, P. and Moore, P., 1974. *Social Work Today.* **5**, 474.

Firth, C. M., 1970. *Quarterly Bulletin of the Research and Intelligence Unit,* Greater London Council, (10), 5.

Firth, C. M., 1971. *Quarterly Bulletin of the Research and Intelligence Unit,* Greater London Council, (17), 5.

Fruin, D., 1976. *BURISA Newsletter,* (21), 2.

Gould, D., 1975. *Municipal and Public Services Journal,* **83**, 861.

Hall, A. S., 1971. *Public Administration,* **49**, 25.

Hamilton, G., 1946. *Principles of social case recording.* New York, Columbia University Press for New York School of Social Work.

Hillingdon. Social Services Department, 1975. *Clearing House for Local Authority Social Services Research,* (2), 43.

Hollis, F., 1967. *Social Casework,* **48**, 489.

Hutton, D. S. S. and Mitchell, H. D., 1974. *Statistical News,* (24). 24.1.

Kane, R. A., 1974. Social Work, (New York), **19**, 412.

Leigh, A., 1973. *New Society,* **23**, 357.

McKane, M., 1975. *Child Welfare,* **54**, 593.

Manchester City Council. Social Services Department, 1975. *Clearing House for Local Authority Social Services Research,* (3), 111.

Mayer, J. E. and Timms, N., 1970. *The client speaks: working class impression of casework.* London, Routledge and Kegan Paul.

Ministry of Health and Department of Health for Scotland, 1959. *Report of the Working Party on Social Workers in the Local Authority Health and Welfare Services.* (Chairman: E. L. Younghusband) London, H.M.S.O.

Moser, C. A., 1971. *The statistician in government: a challenge for the 1970's.* Manchester, Manchester Statistical Society.

Packman, J., 1968. *Child Care: needs and numbers.* (National Institute for Social Work Training Series No. 15) London, Allen and Unwin.

Rowbottom, R. and Hey, A. M., 1970. *Towards an organisation of social services departments.* London, Charles Knight.

Social Services Research Group, 1972. *The preparation of ten year plans,* by John Crook. (S.S.R.G. Paper No. 1) Taunton, Somerset County Council.

Stockbridge, M. E., 1968. *Case Conference,* **15**, 307.

Timms, N., 1968. *The language of social casework.* London, Routledge.

Timms, N., 1972. *Recording in social work.* London, Routledge.

Watts, N., 1974. *Municipal and Public Services Journal,* **82**, 780.

Wright, G. R., 1972. *Child Welfare,* **51**, 182.

Printed in England for Her Majesty's Stationery Office by
Product Support (Graphics) Limited, Derby.
Dd.586504 K16 11/77